PROCESSED FOR PURPOSE

GAIL BURKS-STANSELL

iUniverse, Inc.
Bloomington

Processed For Purpose

iUniverse books may be ordered through booksellers or by contacting:

iUniverse
1663 Liberty Drive
Bloomington, IN 47403
www.iuniverse.com
1-800-Authors (1-800-288-4677)

ISBN: 978-1-4697-4642-5 (sc)
ISBN: 978-1-4697-4643-2 (ebk)

Printed in the United States of America

iUniverse rev. date: 01/26/2012

PROCESSED FOR PURPOSE

Contents

Acknowledgments

God, I thank and praise You for processing me for purpose and giving me the courage I needed to move out of my comfort zone. You are truly awesome!

Anthony Darryl Stansell, my loving husband who supports and encourages me to walk in my destiny. Thank you for the many sacrifices you have made so I can pursue with passion the work God has ordained for my hands.

Brandon Lewis Stansell, you are truly my gift from God and I thank Him for you daily. You make me so proud to call you son. I dedicate this book to you. Let it be a constant reminder that there is nothing too hard for God.

Charlie & Bobbie Lewis, my parents, thank you for the sacrifices you made in my early years so I can now spread my wings and soar.

Dr. Cynthia Worthen, Lillian Burks, Cheryl Dixon, and ***Karen Lewis,*** my siblings, thank you for the valuable life lessons you taught me on perseverance and resilience.

Jody Moore, MA, Senior Pastor of Praise Tabernacle Bible Church, thank you for being my Pastor and spiritual covering during this season of my life. Your passion for ministry and your servant's heart is refreshing and reflected in everything you do.

Cheryl Dixon & Cheryl Hudson, thank you for editing my book and considering it an honor to do so. Words cannot express my gratitude.

Introduction

"Before I formed you in the womb I knew you; Before you were born I sanctified you; I ordained you a prophet to the nations" (Jeremiah 1:5 NKJV).

At the very young age of twelve, I knew God had His hand on me and had called me to do something great during my lifetime. Of course, at twelve years of age I had no idea what it was. It was only after years of trying to figure it out on my own that I finally surrendered. At the point of surrender, God began lovingly moving me out of my comfort zone and placing me in situations where I had to launch out into the deep and tread into unknown waters. It was not long before I found myself desperately seeking the voice of God as I began moving away from barren unproductive things in my life. My inner circle was changing, and it was becoming clearer what God had been calling me to do since the tender age of twelve. This book is one dimension of that calling. It is my prayer that as you read it and prayerfully surrender completely to God, that He will begin lovingly moving you out of your comfort zone so you can walk in His intended purpose for your life.

Chapter One

Purpose in the Process

The butterfly has become the figurative symbol for my life. I have always enjoyed the beauty of butterflies, but never really thought much about the process the butterfly must undergo so I could behold its beauty. Not until August 14, 2006 when I read, *Only A Woman* by Terri McFaddin, did I really begin pondering the process a caterpillar undergoes to transform into a butterfly. In her book, Terri explores the process of a spiritual metamorphosis and compares it to the natural metamorphosis of a caterpillar to a butterfly. The more I thought about the butterfly and each phase of its transformation, I could not help but notice that my own life was transforming. God used the concept of the butterfly's metamorphosis to help me understand the transformation that was taking place in my own life. I was at a point in my life that I needed to hear God's voice in an attempt to understand the struggle taking place within me.

Because of this, I began desperately seeking God. I knew God was real, but He seemed so distant. I was not experiencing His peace. I was actively involved in ministry, faithfully serving in my church, but I was empty.

Well known, loved by all, (or most), but I still felt so alone. Something was happening to me and I could not explain it. All I knew was I was being processed and the transformation was not comfortable, but necessary. I was a caterpillar, destined to become a butterfly. The huge disparity between who I was and who God called me to be before He formed me in my mother's womb presented an enormous conflict within.

The Transformation

From the tiny, seemingly insignificant egg to beautiful unique butterfly, there is a purpose in the process, and each stage is necessary. Butterflies are beautiful; they come in all shapes, sizes, and colors. They are unique; no two will ever be alike. However, before the human eye can ever behold the beauty of a butterfly, it must undergo a meticulous process called metamorphosis or transformation. The transformation takes place in four distinct stages. The process cannot be rushed. There are no shortcuts. Quitting is not an option. In addition, there are no bailouts available. Each stage is necessary to ensure the transformation will take place properly. The butterfly begins life as an egg, emerges as a caterpillar, and transforms into a beautiful butterfly. Although it began as an egg, the butterfly's intended purpose was never to remain an egg, or a caterpillar. Just like the butterfly, God had an intended purpose for my life and He has one for your life too. Although I was in the caterpillar stage, it was not my intended purpose. It was not my destiny. However, it was a necessary step in the process. The "caterpillar stage" of my life was a learning stage. In this stage, I did not really understand and recognize my worth. I did not see my true beauty, or my value. In the caterpillar stage, I did not understand my full potential. In this stage, I, like the caterpillar, was somewhat fuzzy, unsure, slowly moving and inching my way through life. I was afraid to spread my wings and fly. Even when I caught a glimpse of what God had for me, I still doubted. I did not doubt God, but I doubted my ability to achieve what He was showing me.

The Shift

I will praise You, for I am fearfully and wonderfully made;
Marvelous are Your works, And that my soul knows very
well (Psalms 139:14 NKJV).

Suddenly there was a shift in me and I could no longer deny or ignore the greatness within. As the vision for my life became clearer, I no longer wanted to remain a caterpillar. A transformation began in my mind, and I began to see myself as God saw me. The report of the Lord that I was fearfully and wonderfully made was no longer just something I quoted from memory. At this point, I completely embraced and believed Psalm 139:14. I was ready to enter the next phase of the transformation, the "cocoon stage." It is in this stage that the caterpillar uses fine silk threads to encase itself in a cocoon. This encasing serves as a protective covering as the butterfly is developed. Depending on the type of butterfly, the caterpillar can remain in this stage, anywhere from a few weeks to several months. It is in this stage that the transformation takes place.

As it is in the natural, so it is in the spiritual. As I began my process toward purpose, I soon found myself in the cocoon stage, a stage of isolation. In this stage, God will close you in and hide you under the wings of His protective covering. The isolation not only served to keep me in, but it also served to keep out other distractions. During this season, I was not the center of attention. I did not feel much like socializing and small talk. I found myself needing and wanting to be alone. People and things I once enjoyed no longer satisfied me. I started screening my calls, declining invitations, and spending hours in the word of God.

Just like the butterfly, depending on the assignment, the cocoon phase can be a few weeks, a few months, or because a human timetable will not control God, this phase can be several years. During this period of isolation God began making me over. I became clay on the potter's wheel. Before God formed me in my mother's womb, He designated my assignment. God had deposited gifts and talents in me that were critical to my assignment. God would develop me and the gifts during my period of isolation (cocoon phase). Although this phase was uncomfortable, God would not allow me to rush the process. There were no shortcuts, no bailouts, and quitting was not an option. The investment was too great. Besides, God was not concerned about my comfort, He was concerned about His investment. I could not compare my time of processing to the other butterflies around me. I did not have the same assignment, therefore, my processing time would be different.

God will not allow you to stay in the cocoon one second longer than necessary. When it is time to come forth, you will know. Nobody will have to tell you it is time to come forth. Nobody will have to validate you before you can come forth. Nobody will have to give his or her permission when it is time for you to come forth. The preacher will not have to speak a word over you before you come forth. God will let you know when it is time to come out of your cocoon.

God will inspire you to push against the walls of your cocoon when it is time to come forth. God will use different methods to inspire you to push. Sometimes He will use a restless spirit, and at times, He will use situations, things, and people. At other times, God will use losses, hurts, and disappointments to cause you to push against the walls of your cocoon. Over the last several years of my life, I had to make some tough decisions that would ultimately change the course of my life and put me on the path toward my destiny. Each time God used a restless spirit to get my attention.

In his book, *Listening to God*, Dr. Charles Stanley says this about a restless spirit, *"This type of restlessness originates in the deepest aspect of a person's being as part anticipation, part uneasiness. It persists over time."* The anticipation of what I know I heard God say to me caused the restless spirit. Deep down within the recesses of my soul, I felt and heard God calling me. I knew what God had shown me and what God had declared concerning my life. At times, I was somewhat uneasy and downright scared, but I knew it was time to push against the walls of my cocoon and come forth! God was transforming me for such a time as this and I could not allow doubt, fear, and the opinions of others to stop me from pushing and coming forth.

Chapter Two

Your Dream Will Not Die

Now Joseph had a dream, and he told it to his brothers; and they hated him even more. So he said to them, "Please hear this dream, which I have dreamed: There we were, binding sheaves in the field. Then behold, my sheaf arose and also stood upright; and indeed your sheaves stood all around and bowed down to my sheaf." And his brothers said to him, "Shall you indeed reign over us? Or shall you indeed have dominion over us?" So they hated him even more for his dreams and for his words (Genesis 37:5-8 NKJV).

- Is there a dream buried deep within you?
- Do you have a yearning to do something that you have never done?
- What is happening with your dream?
- Are you too afraid to launch out and pursue your dream?

- Has your dream been crushed by doubters or haters?
- Have the circumstances of life caused you to put your dream on hold?

Before God begins processing you for purpose, He will give you a dream. God gave me a dream, but I mistakenly allowed fear, input from others, and the circumstances of life to bury the dream. When I was asked to speak at a woman's conference dealing with this topic, I thought my dream had died. I soon discovered the dream was not dead; and God would use an invitation to speak at a conference to stir up the dream. I do not care what it looks like. I do not care how you feel. I do not care what people said about your dream, or how long it has been since the inception of your dream, your dream will not die. In his book, *The Dream Giver,* Bruce Wilkinson says, *"Everyone has a dream. You may not be able to describe it, you may have forgotten it, but it is there."*

This is what I shared with the women at that conference: Genesis Chapter 37 tells the story of a dreamer name Joseph. Joseph was seventeen years old when he began to dream of better things for his life. He would not spend his entire life tending his father's sheep and collecting wheat. Joseph was not complaining, nor was he ungrateful. After all, he had a job, he was living in the promise land, and he was the favored son, with a brand new elaborate, colorful coat. He had a good life, better than most. However, what do you do when God deposits a dream, a vision for your life deep down in your spirit? No matter what you do and how much you have acquired materially, the dream will not go away. You can change jobs and it does not go away. You can shop until you drop and the dream does not go away. Go back to school and the dream does not go away. Get older and it does not go away. Get married, separated, or even divorced and it does not go away. Buy a new house (the one you always wanted) and the dream is still there. No matter what you do, your dream will not die!

Joseph saw himself in a position of leadership, power, and authority. Even though he was in the field, tending sheep and bundling wheat, in his mind he visualized something very different. What is it that God has shown you? What do you see in your mind and feel in your spirit? Your current location or situation is not your final destination. It is only a temporary layover on your journey towards your destiny. The time you spend in the field, as Joseph did, is necessary for your development, defining your charter and preparing you for what you cannot handle right now. Joseph would one day be second in command, in control of the day-to-day business of an entire nation. At seventeen years old, Joseph was in no way ready for that position. His time in the field would serve to develop his leadership skills and character. Just like Joseph, the fields of your life are necessary for your development. Do not become weary in your fields. They are preparing you for what you cannot handle right now.

In his excitement, Joseph shared his dream with his brothers. You would think Joseph's brothers, his flesh and blood, those who knew him and said that they love him, would be happy for him. The Bible reports a different response. When Joseph told his dream to his brothers, their hatred of him grew worse *(See Genesis 37:5).* This tells me they already had a problem with Joseph, the dream just made matters worse. Be very careful with whom you share your dreams. Not everybody can handle the vision God has given you for your life, especially if it means you will leave him or her behind tending sheep and bundling wheat. Sometimes even the ones who love you cannot handle your dreams. Even when Joseph told his father the dream God had placed in his heart, his father rebuked him. What is a dreamer to do? He was not trying to disrespect his father, nor offend his brothers. Perhaps everybody would have been okay as long as Joseph remained in the field tending sheep, as long as the dream included them, as long as his dream was not larger than their dream, as long as the dream did not venture beyond the expected. Maybe if the dream did not go against the norms or challenge the system, then possibly Joseph's dream would have been acceptable. If Joseph's dream fell into the expectations of his father and his brothers, maybe then Joseph would have received the stamp of approval from them.

To all the dreamers reading this book, you cannot afford to take that chance with your dream. Just make sure your dream is from God. From this day forward, do not feel obligated to explain your dream. Do not look for approval in the planning stages of your dream, and do not try to defend your dream. The battle is not yours anyway, it belongs to God. He is the one who gave you the dream. Do not minimize your dream. In fact, since God is the originator of your dream, the one who placed it in your spirit, you can't alter it anyway. If God said you would own the field instead of tending the field, then that is what you should prepare for. Do not minimize the dream just because it seems impossible from where you stand right now. *All things are possible to him that believes (See Mark 9:23).* For every dreamer there will come a time when you get a clear revelation from God concerning your dream, and it will not match your current situation or position. The dream is bigger than your current situation. Currently, you are tending the fields, but in your dream you own the field. In your present situation, you are following, but in your dream you are the one leading. Joseph's current situation did not match his revelation from God. At times, yours will not either. Because of the dissimilarity, it is hard for onlookers to believe your dream. Just remember, the dream is yours and not the onlookers. Your dream will not die!

Your Dream is Not Without a Cost

Having a dream causes those without dreams and vision to resort to extreme measures to take out the dreamer in an attempt to kill the dream. Joseph's brothers plotted to kill him and then told a lie to their father about what happened to Joseph. Because Joseph revealed his dream to the wrong people, they threw him in a pit and sold him for twenty pieces of silver. What Joseph's brothers did not know was their actions, as horrible as they were, were necessary and part of God's plan. The very actions his brothers meant for harm and destruction, God turned them around for good. God is always in all things working it out for our good *(See Romans 8:28).*

Even though Joseph would experience great pain, sleepless nights, and separation from his family, all at the hands of his brothers, their ill treatment of Joseph all worked together for good and propelled him closer to his dream. Even in a strange land, far from his comfort zone, the Bible says, the Lord was with Joseph and blessed him greatly. In pursuit of your dream, God will put you in the right place at the right time. He will connect you with people you would never have been able to meet on your own. These same people will be another arrow that will propel you closer to your dream.

Even in the midst of blessings and favor, there will be some setbacks, but your dream will not die. Even when it appears your dream is over, and there is no life left in your dream, your dream will not die. Joseph was thrown into prison on false accusations, but his dream did not die. Even in prison, the Lord was with Joseph and granted him favor with the chief jailer. Before long, the jailer put Joseph in charge of the entire prison. Day-to-day operations were under his authority. This was not the conclusion of his dream. Yes, it was a promotion, but it was not his destiny. It was not large enough. It was not what God had originally showed him. *God is able to do exceedingly, abundantly above all, we ask or think . . . (See Ephesians 3:20).* Do not settle for any less than God's best while in pursuit of your dream.

While in prison, Joseph encountered another divine connection, another arrow that would propel him closer to his dream, another holy hookup. Pharaoh, the king of Egypt had a chief cupbearer, who was also a dreamer. The cupbearer had a dream that he did not understand. Joseph interpreted his dream. In the course of trying to figure out your dream, God will often put you in the company of other dreamers who will assist you with your dream. Be very careful how you treat other dreamers. Take heed that you do not crush their dreams, or laugh at their dreams. God may use that very person to launch you to the next level of your dream, as He did with Joseph. Two years after interpreting the dream of Pharaoh's cupbearer, Pharaoh (the king of Egypt) had a dream and the cupbearer remembered Joseph. As you pursue your dream, God will cause people to remember you and give you favor in their eyes. Pharaoh, the king of Egypt, was overjoyed after hearing Joseph interpret his dream. The king appointed Joseph second in command to manage his house and organize his people. Only the king ranked higher than Joseph. At thirty years of age, Joseph had a leadership position equivalent to that of a vice president, and it all started with a dream when he was seventeen years old. It was not easy, he had to overcome some obstacles, but he just kept telling himself, "My dream will not die!"

In his father's field, tending sheep, and gathering wheat, his dream did not die. Hated by his brothers, thrown in a pit, sold into slavery, his dream still did not die. Falsely accused, thrown into prison, the dream lived on.

Thirteen years from revelation to manifestation, but his dream did not die, and yours will not either.

After sharing this message with the women at the conference, I realized it had two things to do with them: little and nothing. God used this speaking engagement as an opportunity to speak to me. Although the women at the conference were there through God's divine purpose to receive a word from the Lord, I began to realize the whole purpose of the speaking engagement was for me. The word was for the dream God had given me while in my cocoon stage. His word to me that day was, "Gail, your dream will not die!"

Chapter Three

Favor Will Move you from Lo Debar to the King's Table

Second Samuel Chapter 9 tells a story of David's kindness towards Mephibosheth, the son of Jonathan and the grandson of Saul. The Bible says David wanted to extend kindness to anyone left in the house of Saul, not for Saul's sake, but for the sake of Jonathan. David and Jonathan had entered into a covenant of friendship and protection that was to extend to their offspring. It was not a normal thing for the current king on the throne to show favor to the family of the previous king. In fact, in that day, it was customary that when a king took the throne he would often eliminate the family of the king before him.

Uncommon Favor from Uncommon People

As the story opens in Second Samuel Chapter 9, we find David showing favor and kindness to Mephibosheth, someone who, according to custom, should have been eliminated. (God will use the most unlikely people to show you uncommon favor while processing you for purpose). Well, David found out that there is a descendent of Saul left and he is living in Lo Debar. When David finds out where the descendent was residing he did not go and get him. I found that very interesting and peculiar that David did not go to Mephibosheth, who was in the land of Lo Debar. After all, David wanted to show kindness. David inquired about Mephibosheth. Mephibosheth was minding his own business, satisfied living in Lo Debar. Mephibosheth was cripple in both feet. Wouldn't it have been easier for David to go to Lo Debar rather than have Mephibosheth come out of Lo Debar? After all, Mephibosheth had a good excuse; he had some issues that kept him in Lo Debar. His nurse had dropped him when he was a child and now he was lame and cripple in both feet. He had family issues. When Mephibosheth was a young child, his father Jonathan and his uncles died at the hands of the Philistines. His grandfather Saul fell on his own sword in an attempt to take his life *(See 1Samuel Chapter 31)*. Mephibosheth had issues that probably made it easier just to stay in Lo Debar.

Just like Mephibosheth, we could probably all argue that we have some issues in our lives that would make it easier to stay where we are. Perhaps, Mephibosheth is not the only one whose nurse dropped them as a child. Your "nurse" is that person who is supposed to protect you, keep you safe, comfort you, console you when you were hurt, and provide for you. Well, just like the nurse of Mephibosheth, your nurse did the best they could under the circumstances. Forgive your nurse so you can move from Lo Debar to the king's table. Your nurse dropping you may not be what keeps you in Lo Debar. Perhaps, other dysfunctional behaviors keep you in Lo Debar. Was it the addiction or the absence of a parent? Did someone take your innocence without your consent? Do you struggle with low self-esteem that has caused you to do things you really did not want to do? Did you grow up way too fast? Were you a mother before you were a bride? Perhaps you took a visit to the clinic because you were not ready to become a mother. Did you settle for ill treatment and disrespect from others because you did not know your real worth and understand that you deserved better?

Perhaps your reason for staying is the same as mine. I stayed because of fear. I was afraid to launch out into the deep. I was afraid of the unknown. I knew what was in Lo Debar, but I did not know what awaited me if I left. I kept asking myself, "What if what I walk into is worse than Lo Debar?" "What if I don't succeed outside of Lo Debar?" "What will be said if I leave Lo Debar?" "Will I be embraced outside of Lo Debar?" At some point, the pain and energy needed to stay in Lo Debar was too much, and I was no longer willing to make the sacrifice, especially when I could feel and hear God pulling me towards greatness. I do not know what your issues are, or why you choose to stay in Lo Debar but I do know this, there is no excuse good enough to stay when the king is knocking at your front door with an invitation to destiny.

The Dangers of Living in Lo Debar

Issues and all, you must come out of Lo Debar! I believe David did not go into Lo Debar because he knew the dangers of living and hanging out in a place called Lo Debar. The Bible says David sent for Mephibosheth and had him brought out of Lo Debar *(See 2 Samuel 9:5)*. You may be asking, "What's so wrong with Lo Debar?" Well, let us begin with the geographical location of Lo Debar. Lo Debar is located about ten miles south of the Sea of Galilee, just east of the Jordan River. This means Lo Debar is physically located outside the borders of the promised land. It is located outside of the promises of God for your life. It is located outside purpose and destiny. Lo Debar is not the will of God for your life.

Secondly, Lo Debar means a place of no pasture, a place of no word or no promise. It is a barren place where not much grows. Barren means it is unproductive, unfruitful, bleak, deserted, and isolated. God's will is not for you to stay in Lo Debar, a place that is located just on the other side of God's promises, blessings, and His favor for your life. Just as God told Jeremiah, He says to you today, *"For I know the thoughts that I think toward you, says the Lord, thoughts of peace and not of evil, to give you a future and a hope" (Jeremiah 29:11 NKJV)*. Before God formed you in your mother's womb, He knew you. Before you were born, He had already set you apart. Your purpose in life was already determined before He formed you. God created you with purpose in mind; a tailor-made purpose just for you. This is why you cannot compare your cocoon stage to the other butterflies around you. This is why you cannot look at what God is doing with someone else and wonder why He didn't do that with you. This is why your life will be totally unique and a personal experience that God planned ONLY for you. You will not experience purpose living in Lo Debar.

When you stay in Lo Debar too long, you develop a negative self-image that leads to negative self-talk. When somebody tries to love you and show you kindness, and favor, you do not know how to accept it. Why? Because you have been in Lo Debar far too long. In Lo Debar, where they do not love, they do not have a kind word for you. In Lo Debar, you are condemned, convicted and criticized because of your issues. If you are living in Lo Debar, it is killing you. It is killing your dreams, your self-worth and your future.

In response to David's acts of favor and kindness, Mephibosheth responded with criticisms of himself. "*Then he bowed himself, and said, "What is your servant, that you should look upon such a dead dog as I" (2 Samuel 9:8 NKJV)?* When you stay in barren, unproductive, unfruitful places (Lo Debar) too long, you become a product of your environment. You begin to see yourself and say about yourself what others see and say about you. You must come out of Lo Debar!

What is your Lo Debar? For Mephibosheth, it was a town just east of the Jordan, outside of the will of God. Yours may not be where you live, but you do have a Lo Debar place or situation that is robbing you of your destiny. Your Lo Debar may be relationships that you are currently involved in, relationships that are outside of the will of God. Well, maybe that is not your Lo Debar. Perhaps your Lo Debar is your job. You may be in a job that is barren, unproductive, and unfruitful. It is not the will of God for your life. Lo Debar is any situation, place, thing, or person that does not allow you to spread your wings and fly. Lo Debar is anything that has you operating beneath your God-given potential and privileges. Lo Debar is anything that keeps you from dreaming and having clear vision and direction. God says to you as He said to me, "It is time to come out!"

Take a few minutes and identify the Lo Debar situation (dry, barren, unproductive) in your life. If you don't know what it is, take a few minutes to pray and ask God to reveal it to you. *Ask and you shall receive. Seek and you shall find (See Matthew 7:7).* God will reveal your Lo Debar situation to you if you ask Him.

_____

_____

_____

_____

_____

_____

The King Is Waiting

When you choose to remain in Lo Debar, you are choosing to live beneath your rights and privileges. There is an empty seat at the king's table with your name on it, and you have been slumming in Lo Debar. It is time for you to come out. Mephibosheth was allowed to eat at the table like one of the king's sons and he still had some issues (See 2 Samuel 9:11 & 13). Do not miss what happened in these verses. Mephibosheth, invited to come out of Lo Debar, takes a seat at the king's table, and he was still lame in both feet. Wow! What a powerful message. We will bring some issues to the table, but we are still welcome.

Do not be afraid to come out of Lo Debar even if you have to come out with the scars as reminders of what happened to you while in Lo Debar. Still come out. The king has reserved a seat for you at the table. He wants to show you kindness and favor. The king wants to bring you to His table where you will always have your needs met according to His riches and glory. The king wants to bring you into His house around His table where you will not be an outcast because of your issues, but the king will lovingly restore you to wholeness. Anybody can come out of Lo Debar. It does not matter if it is your first trip out or if the king had to come get you out several times before. He is a king of another chance. The wait is over; it is time to come out of Lo Debar.

The Invitation from the King

I could not close this chapter without extending the invitation from the king. I believe this book will end up in the hands of persons who have never said yes to the king's invitation to come out of Lo Debar. For that person, your Lo Debar is a life separated from God. A life where there is no real peace or joy, a life on a downward spiral with no ability of your own to control it. A life filled with wilderness wondering with no assurance of ever reaching your destination. It does not have to end like that; today there is an invitation for you. *"That if you confess with your mouth the Lord Jesus and believe in your heart that God has raised Him from the dead, you will be saved. For whoever calls on the name of the Lord shall be saved" (Romans 10:9 & 13 NKJV).*

This is your invitation and promise from the king. No matter who you are. No matter what you have done. Your issues can never cancel out the invitation. Nothing will make the king change His mind about you and the invitation. If you are ready to come out of your Lo Debar, simply pray this prayer:

Dear God, I thank You for sending Your Son Jesus Christ. I believe Jesus was who He said He was and proved it by dying and rising from death. I want to get to know You personally so I can live for You from this day forward. Please forgive me for all my sins. I invite You to come into my life and I give You permission to make me into that person of greatness You created me to be. Thank You, Jesus, for dying for me and forgiving all my sins. I receive You as my Lord and Savior. Thank You for your gift of eternal life. Amen. Welcome to the King's Table!

Chapter Four

Moving Out Of Your Comfort Zone

As God begins processing you for purpose, you will soon discover that where you are no longer fits the person you are becoming. Although it may appear to be a place of comfort, it is actually a dangerous place. It is a place where you no longer hear the voice of God or experience His presence. Your comfort zones are the repeated behaviors and activities you engage in to ensure you do not have to make any changes, take any risks, or become uncomfortable. Let me explain how that translates.

Comfort Zone(s) in Your Life

- Anything you are holding on to although you know there is no potential in it; in fact, it has become counterproductive.
- The point in your life you became stuck in a rut.
- The place in your life when you are too afraid to move forward, but you have come too far to turn back, so you just stay put.
- The things you are tolerating because you are afraid to launch out into the deep.

- The things you would let go of or move away from if you knew you would not fail.

- The relationships in your life that should have ended a long time ago.

- The place you are settling for because you have given up on your dreams.

Now, before you read another page, take a few minutes and identify areas of your life that have become a comfort zone.

_____

_____

_____

_____

_____

_____

_____

_____

_____

_____

_____

_____

_____

_____

_____

_____

_____

_____

_____

_____

_____

If you choose to remain in your comfort zone, you will pay a heavy price. The price may not be in terms of dollars and cents, but you will have to pay in one way or another. One of the many ways you pay is an inner turmoil, or restlessness that will cause you to forfeit the peace of God in your life. In January 2006, I began to experience restlessness in my sprit that literally consumed me. I knew God was trying to move me out of a comfort zone. I had been in this place before; I knew the signs of a restless spirit. I knew what God was saying to me. I knew He was using a restless spirit to get my attention, but fear of the unknown paralyzed me. As I began writing this book, I pulled out my journals from that period in my life. I want to share several journal entries that speak to the restlessness I was experiencing during that season.

Journal Entry: May 4, 2006 at 11:25AM

I do not know what is going on but I am in that restless place, needing to be alone stage, not completely alone but just away from certain people and situations. I am weepy again, seeking purpose, and meaning. I am not sleeping well. I just want to hear the word of God all day. The last time I felt this way was right before I answered the call to ministry. I just feel like I am on the verge of something great. I do not know what to do. I do not want to get in my own way. God, I need You to guide and lead me. Do what You want in my life. I feel like You are shaping and molding me for a great assignment and I ask for guidance, direction, and wisdom. You said if I lack wisdom just ask. God I am asking, please give me wisdom and discernment in this situation. I do not want to move unless You say move. I do not want to stay if You are telling to me to move. Show me Your will for my life in this.

Journal Entry: May 5, 2006 at 10:45AM

I am at work and I cannot even focus on work. My mind is on God; my heart is on God. I am definitely in labor again. The feeling is the same; the intensity is just as great or greater. God is trying to birth something through me and I just want to bring it forth . . . God, I feel You are confirming in my spirit what my heart and head already knows. In the natural birthing process once labor begins you are uncomfortable, there is a fear of the unknown, and restlessness. God, it feels like I am at that point in my life. I feel like I am at the threshold of something . . .

Journal Entry: February 2, 2007 at 10:10AM

I am at work and feeling so empty. I thank God for my job, but I know there is so much more that is required of me. I know God has called me to do so much more. He has called me to be a world changer. I know I am changing lives even on this level, but I know there is so much more God has called me to do. I am not satisfied with this. There has to be more. I can just feel it . . .

For nearly two years, I experienced a restless spirit that left me feeling frustrated and confused. I believe my settling for less and refusing to move out of my comfort zone caused the frustration and the restless spirit. I knew the call on my life. I knew God had plans to give me a hope and a future and I was settling for less than my intended destiny. It was not until I said yes to God and began allowing Him to lead me out of my comfort zone that I truly experienced the peace of God that passes all understanding.

Desperate People do Desperate Things

At some point in your life, you must become so desperate to walk in God's perfect will for your life that you are willing to do whatever it takes to achieve it. I am talking about the kind of desperation that causes you to challenge protocol, traditions, and the opinions of others. There will come a time when something deep down inside of you will rise up and shout, "I am too desperate for protocol!"

Mark Chapter 5 tells the story of a woman whom I believe one day woke up and shouted, "I am too desperate for protocol!" For twelve years, she had tried protocol and that did not work. She had tried rules and correct procedures, and that did not work. She had tried proper etiquette, and that did not work. By now, this woman was too desperate for protocol. So out of her desperation she interrupted Jesus' next scheduled appointment *(See Mark 5:21-28)*. At this point, she did not care that Jesus' next scheduled appointment was with the ruler of the synagogue, and she was just a nameless woman in the crowd who was too desperate for protocol because protocol had failed her.

This woman had suffered a great deal under the care of many doctors and had spent all she had; yet instead of getting better, she grew worse. I can hear this woman saying, don't tell me another thing about protocol! Been there, done that, and it did not work. The very people that she thought would help her, hurt her. In fact, the Bible says, instead of getting better, she got worse. So, not only was this woman worse physically, mentally, and emotionally, she was broke and frustrated, all behind following protocol.

When you find yourself in a desperate situation (and you will), you have to resort to desperate measures. You have to do things out of the ordinary. Things you would never do if the situation were different. Like the woman in Mark Chapter 5, after twelve years you stop caring about what people in the crowd say or think. You are too desperate to care. What you need, nobody in the crowd has anyway! What you need is bigger than the crowd is. What you need is bigger than where you are now; this is why God has to move you out of your comfort zone. He has to move you to grow you. The next level of your life is contingent upon you moving out of your comfort zone.

The Touch of Desperation

"And Jesus, immediately knowing in Himself that power had gone out of Him, turned around in the crowd and said, "Who touched My clothes" (Mark

5:30 NKJV)? The touch of desperation is unlike any other touch. When you are truly ready to move out of your comfort zone, your touch will be the sign. Your touch will not be the same way you touched Jesus in the past. Your touch will cause Jesus to stop and ask, "Who touched me?" His disciples must have thought Jesus was crazy. I mean, think about it, there are hundreds of people pushing and shoving trying to get close to Jesus, and he stops and asks, "Who touched me?" The touch of desperation is different from any other touch.

Sure, there were others in the crowd who touched Jesus, but something was different about this woman's touch. Her reason for coming was different. Everybody in the crowd didn't come because they were desperate and wanted to move out of their comfort zone. Some came just to see if Jesus was really all that. Some came just to have something to gossip about later. Some came to judge and ridicule. I am sure some in the crowd came just to socialize. I do not know, perhaps some came because they had a new outfit and needed a place to wear it. Let's face it, not everybody in the crowd came for the same thing.

When you get ready to move, you will do whatever it takes to touch Him. You will not wait for an invitation. You will show up in places without an invitation just because you heard Jesus was passing by. You will push your way through the crowd with a determination in your spirit that says, "I will not leave until I touch Him!" You will interrupt scheduled appointments when you are ready to move. When this desperate woman entered the picture in Mark Chapter 5, Jesus was on His way to attend to the daughter of Jairus, who was at the point of death. However, the woman interrupted His next scheduled appointment. When was the last time you were so desperate to touch Jesus that you interrupted your day to meet with Him?

Understanding the Move

Your move will not be without some opposition. Just because you are ready to move, it does not mean everybody and everything in your life is just going to come in alignment and allow you to move without resistance. Expect resistance! Expect some murmuring and complaining from others in the crowd. If you are ready to move out of your comfort zone, here are some helpful tips.

Ignore People Who Cannot Help You & Believe in the One Who Can

In the same chapter *(See Mark 5:35)* as Jesus began to make His way to the home of Jairus, someone announced that Jesus did not even need to show up because Jairus' daughter was already dead. It is very interesting to me that people who did not give life to your dreams, hopes and visions often feel they have the power to pronounce death over them. However, Jesus teaches a lesson that you cannot afford to miss as you begin to move out of your comfort zone. *As soon as Jesus heard the word that was spoken,*

He said to the ruler of the synagogue, "Do not be afraid; only believe" (Mark 5:36 NKJV).

Jesus never addressed the reports that came from the crowd. He did not waste time correcting, debating, or even engaging in a conversation with them. He turned and spoke directly to Jairus. You must learn to ignore the people who cannot help you. Do not waste time engaging in conversation with people who do not have the ability or the desire to help you. The first thing Jesus said to Jairus was, "Do not be afraid." Jesus knows that the fear in your heart will paralyze you and you will never move out of your comfort zone. I believe this is why it is the first thing He addresses. Do not be afraid of what people are saying. Do not be afraid of what it looks like. It's not over! Do not be afraid of your lack of resources. If He leads you there, (wherever there is), He will provide for you there. Do not be afraid of your age; it is not too late. Do not be afraid of what they have said about your situation, about your dreams, nor about the vision God has shown you for your life. Do not be afraid; only believe! Jesus says, *"If you can believe, all things are possible to him who believes" (Mark 9:23 NKJV)*. Ignore people who cannot help you and believe in the one who can.

You Need an Inner Circle

As God begins processing you for purpose, you will need an inner circle. Not crowds, just a small group who can support you and speak into your life on days you want to quit. Directly after Jesus finish speaking to Jairus, He permitted no one to follow Him except Peter, James and John *(See Mark 5:37)*. Why were the other disciples and the people who came from the house to deliver the news not allowed to follow Jesus? The Bible does not say, but in my own experiences I have discovered when it's time to move, you must pack lightly and be prepared to move quickly. Extra baggage will cost you. You do not need the baggage of doubters who are quick to say, "Stop troubling Jesus because the situation is dead." You do not need a bunch of extra folks that cause you to stop and explain your every move. You have wasted enough time explaining your dreams to folks who do not believe. You will need an inner circle. People in your inner circle are those who can pray with you, and those who can believe with you. They can see the vision in the spiritual long before it manifests in the natural. Your inner circle consists of individuals who are just as excited about your move as you are. It may only be two or three people, but that is all you will need.

You Will Have To Put Some People Out

There will come a time when you find it necessary to put some people completely out of your life. It does not mean you do not love them. It does not mean you are angry with them. It does not mean you will delete them from your prayer list. It simply means there are some in your life now who cannot go with you. They may have been good for where you were, but they are not ready for where you are going. They cannot handle the call on your life. In fact, they may have laughed when you told them what God spoke to you regarding your destiny. It is okay. Let them laugh. Just do what Jesus did when they laughed at Him. *"But they laughed at him. After he put them all out, he took the child's father and mother and the disciples who were with him, and went in where the child was" (Mark5:40 NIV).* If Jesus had to put some people out, surely you will have to put some people out of your life. So let them laugh and doubt you. When you get to your final destination, you will look back and say, "Look who's laughing now?"

You Can Still Move Even If It Appears Too Late

No matter the stage in your life, you can still pack your bags and move. Jesus still has the last word! *Then He took the child by the hand, and said to her,* "Talitha, cumi," *which is translated, "Little girl, I say to you, arise" (Mark 5:41 NKJV).* Jesus really does have the last word concerning your life. I do not care who has tried to pronounce death over your dreams and destiny before He showed up. It appeared that the girl was dead, as if all her dreams had ended, all while waiting for Jesus to show up. The folks had already gathered for the funeral. Perhaps already shouting, "I told you so!" "I knew He would not come through for you!" "I knew it was a fantasy and not a vision from God!" People are quick to have your funeral and bury your dreams. Do not let them do it! Wait for the last word from Jesus. Listen for His instructions, "Talitha, cumi" (translation), "Get up girl!" It is moving day! Pack your bags and follow Him. It is time to move out of your comfort zone.

Chapter Five

Speak God I am Listening

On January 11, 2007 at 11:30 PM, I wrote this in my journal. *God, you have said yes and I thank you. As I sit here, thinking about confirmation that God has said yes and given His stamp of approval, this is what I hear the Holy Spirit speaking to my heart. There will be a peace about the situation. It will appear that plans are coming together effortlessly. God will connect you to resources (people and situations). Favor will surround you like a shield. Gail, whatever you do will prosper.*

I did not understand it all at the time but now five years later I know God was speaking and reassuring me that He was, in fact, leading me, and that He would never leave me. During my wilderness season, God was truly speaking, and I am so glad I had an ear to hear. While in my wilderness season, I literally slept with my journal. I used it to record my thoughts, prayers, concerns, fears, doubts, and especially those times God spoke to me. When I began writing this book, I pulled out my journals from a period in my life when I was desperately seeking to hear from God. It was amazing to see how God spoke to me. I want to use this chapter to share some of those entries in hopes that you will see how God speaks loud and clear, when we are ready to hear. I do not claim to be an expert on how God speaks, nor am I limiting the ways God speak. He is God. He can do what He wants to do, how He wants to do it, when He wants to do it. However, during my wilderness season as God processed me for purpose, He spoke to me in several primary ways.

God Spoke Through Scripture

During my season of seeking, searching, listening, and desperately needing to hear the voice of God above all others, I noticed four recurring scriptures. When I say "recurring," I literally mean recurring. I would read from my daily devotion and one of the scriptures would appear. I would hear a sermon and one of the scriptures would be included. I would get an email from a friend and they would reference one of the scriptures. I would be reading a book and the author would reference one of the scriptures. For a period of two months, June 19, 2006 to August 26, 2006, these four scriptures became the constant and consistent message God spoke to me. The first scripture, "*I will instruct you and teach you in the way you should go; I will guide you with My eye*" (*Psalm 32:8 NKJV*). Wow, what assurance this was for me. I was in the middle of a life-changing decision, which would affect every area of my life. I needed clarity, direction, and instructions. God was reminding me through His word that He would instruct me on the way I should go. Not only would He instruct me, but also He would guide me with His eye. This was exactly what I needed to hear during a time when I was scared to death to take a step. Fear had paralyzed me. What would they say? What would they think? Could I really move out of my comfort zone and succeed? I had so many questions, and although God did not provide the answers at that very moment, He did give me a word of assurance that He would be navigating my course.

The second scripture, "*But without faith it is impossible to please Him, for he who comes to God must believe that He is, and that He is a rewarder of those who diligently seek Him*" (*Hebrews 11:6 NKJV*). God told me He would instruct me and guide me, but now He was asking me to make the first move. He could not lead where I was not willing to follow. He had a plan for my life and if I was going to walk in it, I had to move. Destiny was calling and I had to take a bold leap of faith to answer it. I had preached about faith, talked about faith, taught on faith, I had encouraged others to walk in faith, and now it was time for a test on all that faith talk. God was clearly saying to me, if I wanted to please Him, I would have to walk by faith and not by sight. I could not go any further unless I was willing to take a bold leap of faith. I wanted so badly for God to show me a sign, to show me the place He was leading, to give me a clue. I pleaded with Him, I tried to bargain with Him, but it did not move Him. No matter how hard I pleaded and bargained, it would not change what God said. At this point, I either had to be willing to take the bold leap of faith and come out of Lo Debar (which was a comfort zone) or miss destiny moments. I am so glad I took that leap of faith.

The third scripture, *"For with God nothing will be impossible"* (*Luke 1:37 NKJV*). God did not show me the exact place He was leading; however, He did promise nothing was impossible with Him. Boy, did I need this one! I do not care how much fear I had, it was no match for this scripture. God was speaking to me loud and clear. Nothing would be impossible with Him. Every dream, everything He had spoken to me, I would do it! I would achieve it! I would write the book! I would present the workshop series in every state! I would lead women to God by telling my story! My gift would make room for me! I would be a world changer for God, changing lives one woman at a time! I would be able to give out of my overflow! I would be a blessing to crowds large and small all over this world as I shared with them the love of God! I would be in good health, mind, body, and spirit! I would leave my job for full-time ministry! Nothing would be impossible with God!

The fourth scripture, *"Therefore if anyone cleanses himself from the latter, he will be a vessel for honor, sanctified and useful for the Master, prepared for every good work"* (*2 Timothy 2:21 NKJV*). God was telling me to get ready. He had a plan to use me for His glory. He was calling me to be a world changer and I needed to be ready. I needed to be a vessel of honor prepared for every good work. My walk needed to match my talk. I needed to make sure I was pursuing Him and righteousness, and not things. I needed to make sure that the people, places, and things in my life enhanced my witness. Where God was taking me, I could not afford to attach to things that would distract or destroy my witness. As I look back on it now, I needed to be ready for all situations, for all types of ministry. God was about to take me to places I needed to be persuasive and confident enough to minister to the divas of the world, but I also needed to have the credibility and transparency to minister to the addict and the prostitute. My life would be on public display. I could not risk missing an opportunity to speak into the lives of the countless people who would cross my path. God was preparing me to be a vessel of honor for His use.

God Spoke Through a Sermon

This is a journal entry taken from July 7, 2006 at 9:39PM. *Tonight I heard a sermon on Trinity Broadcast Network (TBN) preached by Bishop T.D. Jakes. The message was dealing with hearing the voice of God. I do not know the title because when I turned on the television the program was already in progress. The scripture reference was Genesis 22: 1-14. The following are excerpts from that sermon that God used to speak directly to me.*

- *"When you get to the place you are supposed to be, you will know."*
- *"You are being pulled toward destiny."*
- *"God did not give Abraham details."*
- *"There is a place in the journey when the people who started with you, will not end with you. They are not ready to go with you so kiss them good-bye."*

- *"Doing God's will, will take you from your comfort zone to a place of uncertainty."*
- *"God Himself will provide what you will need to get the job done."*
- *"Abraham could not see the answer, but the answer was coming. It will be there when you get there."*
- *"God already has a plan worked out from the foundation of the world."*

The words I heard from God's servant on July 7, 2006 was exactly what I needed, at exactly the right time. I am convinced God ordered my steps and led me to turn on the television at that precise moment. Not only was it a powerful message of confirmation, but also it was timely. Just twenty-four hours prior, I had a conversation with an individual who was trying to convince me that perhaps I had not heard from God regarding moving out of my comfort zone and possibly others were influencing my decision. If I had listened to that individual instead of believing what God had already spoken to me, you would not be reading this book. I just want to say, thank you, God, that you did not let me listen to my doubters, and thank you Bishop T.D. Jakes, for a powerful word from God. It was the last arrow I needed to propel me closer to destiny. Wow, I just looked at the date again that I heard the sermon, and could not help but notice it was the seventh month on the seventh day. Seven is God's number for completion. That night marked the completion of my doubting, seeking, and wondering if I had truly heard from God regarding the next move in my life. It was final; I had to move out of my comfort zone.

God Used Other Believers to Confirm He Was Speaking

Noticed I said, "God used other believers to confirm." Be very careful of people who are quick to tell you what God said concerning your life. During my season of seeking God's voice, every time God used someone to speak into my life, it was always a confirmation of something God had already spoken to me. When I began my season of seeking and wilderness journeying, I remember feeling this overwhelming need to journal. The urge was so strong that I found myself carrying my journal with me everywhere I went. On any given day, I would record five to ten entries, sometimes more. For as long as I can remember, I have always written in a journal, but it was not consistent. However, during this season there was not a day that went by that I did not write in my journal. One day, while in my wilderness season, I remember saying to myself, "These journal entries will one day be a workshop series that I will present to women all over the world, and then a book." I knew that came from God. I knew He was telling me to write down everything. Well, a few days later I received a phone call from a friend. Below is the journal entry from that call.

July 26, 2006 at 4:15PM: A friend called me today. She was checking on me to see how I was doing. We shared and talked for a while. I began telling her how I had been in a three-year struggle. I told her I knew it was three years because I had been keeping a journal and it was during our last retreat that I spoke about the pains of developing your relationship with God. She then replied, "You need to hold on to your journals because they will one day become a book." This is the second person that has said this to me. God is able to do exceedingly abundantly above all we ask or think.

These are only a few examples of how God spoke to me during that season. I could literally write a book on just journal entries during my wilderness season. God is speaking. The question is, "Are you listening?" Before you go to the next chapter take a few minutes and write down your thoughts, fears, concerns, or prayers.

Journal Entry:

Date:

Time:

_____

_____

_____

_____

_____

_____

_____

_____

_____

_____

_____

_____

_____

_____

_____

_____

_____

_____

_____

_____

_____

Chapter Six

The Power of Relationships

Jesus had an inner circle. Peter, James, and John often accompanied Jesus during the most difficult and celebrated moments of His life. What type of people do you need in your inner circle? Are the relationships you surround yourself with propelling you or weighing you down? I pray that this chapter challenges you to explore your current relationships and answer this question, "Are the relationships closest to you suitable and intended for where you are going?" The relationships may have been okay for a season, but as God begins processing you for purpose, you will soon discover your inner circle will have to change. Many people that are in your life now cannot handle where God is about to take you. Reading back over my journals, I found so many entries where I was simply praying to God. In those prayers, I asked God on so many occasions to surround me with people who could support me at the next level, and He did exactly that. Take a moment and answer the following questions.

- Do the people in your inner circle support you and provide a safe place for you to be transparent?

- Do the people in your inner circle have dreams, visions, and goals they are actively pursuing?

- Is there someone in your inner circle who can offer wise counsel and lovingly correct you when you get off course?

- Do those in your inner circle inspire you and motivate you to soar to new heights?

- Can those in your inner circle rejoice with you when God is doing amazing things in your life (even if they are in a wilderness season)?

If you cannot answer yes to these questions, you may want to rethink your inner circle. As God began processing me for purpose, I noticed many of my relationships were changing. I was not hanging out with questionable or unsavory people, but something was missing in my relationships. It was not every person in my circle, but there were some. I felt like I could not really shine or walk in my true potential. In some of my relationships, an unspoken tension caused me to shrink so that others could feel secure. I often found myself being the great cheerleader, supporter, and encourager for their projects and dreams, but when I needed that same thing, my cheering section was empty. When I began looking around my circle, I did not feel inspired. Many times, I found myself drained because I had given so much. I loved the people I was in relationship with, but God was trying to show me something. Many of those relationships were fine for where I was, but as God began to shift and transition me, those relationships would no longer be enough. The truth is simply this, the relationships (as wonderful as the people may have been) were not suited for where I was going.

Change in the Inner Circle

The first shift I noticed in my inner circle was God surrounding me with those who comforted and supported me. I did not realize how empty and drained I had become. Teaching, giving, supporting, praying for, advising, and mentoring had burned me out. God needed to prepare me for the journey. So, the first thing He provided in my inner circle was a loving family known for their gift of hospitality. I called them "my personal gifts from God." So many Sunday afternoons I would show up at their doorstep completely empty with nothing else to give because I had given of myself all week long. They greeted me with warm hugs, smiles, kisses, and food. For my tired, weary feet they took my shoes and replaced them with warm, fuzzy slippers or socks. They took my clothes and in exchange, they gave me a cozy robe or housedress, and insisted that I recline in the big comfortable chair. Whether it was a hamburger on the grill, meatloaf or chicken, coffee or dessert, I did not leave that home until my physical body was well fed and my spirit had been encouraged. They did it all, expecting nothing in return except for a promise from me that I would show up the following week. Wow! I could not believe how much God showed His love for me through this family.

Inspired To Be My Best

Have you ever been in the presence of someone who energized and inspired you every time you were in his or her presence? As my circle continued to change, I noticed God rearranging the role of one particular person in my life. It was someone I had known, loved, and supported for years. This person began showing up in my life in a different role. Where I once had the role of encouraging, inspiring and supporting, the roles suddenly reversed. God used this individual to motivate me and challenge me to move out of my comfort zone. The motivation came as I watched them pursue dreams and goals that many believed would be impossible to obtain. We spent hours talking, laughing, and on some occasions even crying, but at the end of each conversation, I was inspired to walk in what God had called me to do. What I did not know at the time was this: God used this individual and their success to inspire me to set my goals higher and truly believe in myself. Every person who is being processed for purpose needs an individual in their circle who inspires them to be their best, no matter what the crowd is saying and the circumstances look like.

Seeing What You Cannot See

Sometimes God will use relationships totally outside your normal circle to help you see the magnitude of your gifts and call. Many times those closest to you are not the ones who celebrate the gifts that God has placed in you. Prior to leaving my job, I worked for a nonprofit counseling agency. During those eight years, God allowed me to work alongside two individuals who helped shape the person I am becoming. The two relationships happened at separate times at the company for whom I was employed. The first person was already there when I was hired and I just "happened" (nothing in the life of a child of God just happens) to get the desk right next to hers. For years, she encouraged me to step out and pursue the dreams I had shared with her. She constantly admired the skills and gifts God had given me. She would often say to me, "You just don't see it!" "You've got what it takes!" She was right; I did not see it (at the time) and I did have what it takes!

Well, fast-forward a few years, the desk next to mine was vacant because my dear friend had moved out of her comfort zone and was now pursuing her passion. Another person was hired to fill the vacancy and this person just "happened" (nothing in the life of a child of God just happens) to take the vacant desk next to me. It was not the only vacant desk in the office, but this person chose that desk. Wow! This person picked up exactly where the other person left off. God knew exactly what I needed and when one person left, He replaced her with what He knew I would still consistently need. He did not leave me nor forsake me. He gave me just who I needed to encourage me to walk where I knew God was telling me to walk. God did not miss a beat nor did the two people who He chose to speak into my life at this time. We spent hours before, during, and after work talking. There was a connection, and a level of support from these two individuals that I was not receiving from some of my closest relationships. They saw in me what I could not see in myself and gave me the boost I needed to soar.

The Power to Soar

In the wilderness, as you move toward destiny, you must understand the power of relationships and the ability relationships have in producing an effect. The relationships you attach yourself to have the ability to cause you to spread your wings and soar, or immobilize you to the point where you never get off the ground. Ask God to surround you with people who can support you during this season of your life. Ask God to surround you with the kind of people who can offer wise counsel and are not afraid to confront and correct when needed. You need relationships that can provide support and encouragement when your current situation does not match your revelation from God. You need people who just want to love and support you and expect nothing in return, but for you to show up the following week so they can do it all over again. God will place people on your path that will help you reach your destiny. Do not miss them hanging out with people who are not ready to soar and do not want to see you soar either!

Chapter Seven

Don't Die In Your Wilderness

"To everything, there is a season, a time for every purpose under heaven" (Ecclesiastes 3:1 NKJV).

Whatever you do, do not die in your wilderness. You are at the threshold of your breakthrough. If you give up now, the enemy will rob you of your testimony and your dream. It is just a season, and seasons do change. Your season has a definite beginning and a definite ending. The things that happen during your wilderness season will test your faith and cause you to wonder if God really does hear your cries. Perhaps understanding the wilderness season will help you press your way to the other side of the wilderness.

A Season of Transition and Shifting

"Then the word of the Lord came to me, saying: Before I formed you in the womb I knew you; Before you were born

I sanctified you; I ordained you a prophet to the nations.

Then said I Ah, Lord God! Behold I cannot speak, for I am

a youth. But the Lord said to me: Do not say, I am a youth,

for you shall go to all to whom I send you, And whatever I

command you, you shall speak" (Jeremiah 1:4-7 NKJV).

Before you were born God had a plan for your life, and nothing you do or say can abort or change that plan. No excuse will cancel the plan. Your delayed obedience cannot even cancel the plan. However, sometimes while on the course of day-to-day living things happen that may alter your course. Just because you get off course, it does not change God's decision regarding the plan for your life. When this occurs, the only thing left to do is shift and transition you so you can realign with God's intended purpose and plan. Causing pain is not the intention of the shift. The intention of the shift is to put you back on course. Now, the intensity and the degree of difficulty caused by the shift will depend totally on you. If you resist, delay, or fight the transition this will cause a greater degree of difficulty and a higher level of intensity. The sooner you surrender and say yes to God's plan, the quicker you can get back on course and proceed toward destiny.

A Season of Labor Pains

In the natural progression of childbirth, the beginning of labor pain indicates the birthing process has begun. As it is in the natural, so it is in the spiritual. The pain you are experiencing in your wilderness season is just an indication the birthing processing has begun. You are pregnant with greatness, and limitless possibilities. There are dreams, talents, and gifts buried deep within you. Many of you are far beyond your due date and this is why the pain is so intense. Your burden is so heavy, and the restlessness you are experiencing is beyond description. In the natural, the pain of labor progress in three distinct phases. While in the wilderness, I discovered my labor season was no different from the natural birthing process. I distinctly remember going through each phase.

The longest phase of labor is called the early phase. Prior to now, you have been able to ignore the pain (restlessness, heavy burdens) because if you reposition yourself, the pain will normally subside for a while. However, when true labor begins the pain does not subside after repositioning. In this phase certain things, situations, and people in your life make you uncomfortable. Your pains are closer together and they last for longer periods. During this phase, you may still be seeking comfort from others and complaining about the frequency and the length of the pains.

The second phase of labor is called the active phase. In this phase, you find yourself needing and wanting to be alone. You are no longer seeking comfort from outside sources. This is the time to focus and listen to your birthing coach (the Holy Spirit).

The final stage before you began to push is the advanced stage of labor (also known as the transitional phase). This phase of labor is the most difficult part of labor. It is during this phase that there is no rest. You cannot tell when one pain ends and another begins. At this point, everybody that is not part of the birthing team (your inner circle) is no longer welcomed in the birthing room. You do not have the strength for unnecessary conversation and distractions. You must save your strength so you can be prepared to push. There is a strong urge to quit because you are very exhausted. You cannot quit at this point. You have come too far. Let me encourage you by telling you this: although the advanced phase (transition) is the most difficult, it is also the shortest phase of labor. You must go through the transition. The transition will shift you so you can move into position to receive what God has for you. He wants to birth something through you. You have been experiencing tailor-made struggles and pains, designed to shift and transition you into position; so bear down and prepare to push!

When the Revelation from God Does Not Match Your Current Situation

In your wilderness season, you will soon discover a huge disparity. While in the wilderness (your current situation), you will notice it does not look, feel, or sound like the revelation you received from God. You know what you heard God say concerning your destiny, but where you are does not match that revelation. There is a simple explanation for this discrepancy. The place you are (the wilderness) is not your final destination. You are just passing through. It is just a season, and seasons do change! It is a layover on your way to destiny. This is the reason it does match the revelation you received from God. The revelation is on the other side of the wilderness, but you must go through the wilderness. While in the wilderness, God showed me I was not fully ready for the revelation He had shown me. Therefore, He used the wilderness season to build my character and strengthen my faith. It was a season of pruning as He prepared me for the assignment that awaited me on the other side of the wilderness. When I went into the wilderness, I had baggage that God would deal with. I had some character defects that would get in the way at the next level, and if God did not smooth them out in my wilderness season, they would have destroyed me at the next level. I had faith before the wilderness, but I believe it was anemic faith. At the next level, I would have to trust God as I walked away from a career that I had worked hard to achieve. I was well—loved and respected in my work, but I would soon be asked to leave and walk in the assignment God had for me. God would soon be asking me to leave a community of believers (my comfort zone) who had watched me grow up. As with Abraham, *(See Genesis 12:1)*. I would be asked to get out of my country, away from my family and from my father's house and go to a land that only God could show me. In the wilderness, I developed the kind of faith I would need at the next level. So, yes, your observation is correct, where you are does not match the revelation you received from God, because you are not where you are going. You are just passing through. Do not get comfortable. Be prepared to move quickly because you are in the advanced stage of labor. It is almost time to push and bring forth what God revealed to you.

Instruction for Your Wilderness Season

- **Wait on the Lord and do not be in a hurry:** *"But those who wait on the Lord shall renew their strength; They shall mount up with wings like eagle, They shall run and not be weary, They shall walk and not faint"* (*Isaiah 40:31 NKJV*). Your waiting time is not wasted time. You have simply paused for further instructions. Wait with a hope, expectancy, and anticipation that God will do exactly what He said He would do. Wait knowing that when God comes to deliver you from the wilderness, He will renew your strength.

- **Worship and give thanks:** *"In everything give thanks; for this is the will of God in Christ Jesus for you"* (*1 Thessalonians 5:18 NKJV*). Thank God for every valley. Thank Him for every hill you had to climb. Thank Him for every person who ever told you no. Thank Him for how He kept you while in the wilderness. Thank Him that you did not lose your mind in the wilderness. Thank Him for not taking you to the next level without processing you in the wilderness first. Thank Him for the lessons you learned in the wilderness. In everything, give Him thanks.

- **Do not forget to write:** Whatever you do, do not forget to journal. Tell your story because it will set you and so many others free.

Conclusion

On your journey toward destiny, you will experience a season of processing that will require you to spend some time in isolation (your cocoon stage). Do not rush the process. Allow God to process you so you can move out of your comfort zone and reap the benefits of a surrendered life. God has shown you a vision for your life, and I know from your current position it may seem as if it will never manifest. Take your eyes off your current position and put them on God. Remember the story of Joseph. There was a thirteen-year period from revelation to manifestation. Your dream will not die. Some days it will appear God has forgotten you in your cocoon stage. Be encouraged, and remember that before you behold the beauty of a butterfly, it must go through its cocoon phase. Just as the butterfly must undergo a meticulous process before it can push against the wall of its cocoon, so must you. It does not yet appear what you shall be, but rest assured God has His hand in it!

Writing this book has been an amazing testimony to the power of journaling. Not only did my journaling serve as a way for me to process my thoughts and communicate with God through my many prayers, it also served as a therapeutic tool, which became the foundation for this book. Anybody who knows me can tell you I am a huge fan of journaling.

I often say journaling was one of the tools God used to help me survive my wilderness season. One of the first questions I ask the many women who share their stories with me is, "Are you writing it down?" Telling your story is necessary, and it begins with writing it down. Before you close this book, take a few minutes and write down your feelings and thoughts on what you have just read. It is my prayer you will begin (or continue) a steady diet of prayer, seeking God for direction, wisdom, and journaling as you are being processed for purpose.

Journal Entry:

Date:

Time:

_____

_____

_____

_____

_____

_____

_____

_____

_____

_____

_____

_____

_____

_____

_____

_____

_____

_____

_____

References

McFaddin, Terri, Only A Woman Claiming Your Amazing Power In Christ (Sisters, Oregon, Multnomah Publishers, Inc., 2001)

Stanley, Charles, Listening To God (Nashville, Tennessee, Thomas Nelson, Inc., 1996)

Wilkinson, Bruce, The Dream Giver (Sisters, Oregon, Multnomah Publishers, Inc., 2003)